TURN LIGHTS ON

How to Light up Your World and Live a Life You Love Now

GEORGINA JONES

Copyright © 2014 Georgina Jones.

All rights reserved. No part of this book may be reproduced, stored, or transmitted by any means—whether auditory, graphic, mechanical, or electronic—without written permission of both publisher and author, except in the case of brief excerpts used in critical articles and reviews. Unauthorized reproduction of any part of this work is illegal and is punishable by law.

ISBN: 978-1-4834-1873-5 (sc)
ISBN: 978-1-4834-1872-8 (e)

Library of Congress Control Number: 2014917086

Because of the dynamic nature of the Internet, any web addresses or links contained in this book may have changed since publication and may no longer be valid. The views expressed in this work are solely those of the author and do not necessarily reflect the views of the publisher, and the publisher hereby disclaims any responsibility for them.

Any people depicted in stock imagery provided by Thinkstock are models,
and such images are being used for illustrative purposes only.
Certain stock imagery © Thinkstock.

Lulu Publishing Services rev. date: 10/24/2014

To the two people in the world who always turn my light on.

To my parents, Anne and Peter Jones from Swansea, Wales. They have always been there for me and supported me in all I have done. They are two wonderful people. I'm so proud to know them and even prouder to call them my parents. Thanks, Mammy and Daddy, for making TLO happen with me.

About the Author

All her life, Georgina Jones has been inspired to ignite a spark in people. From singing on stage to running teams, coaching, or spending five minutes brightening up the day of a stranger, Georgina loves turning people's lights on.

Whether in businesses, communities, or online, it is Georgina's life goal to inspire people, so that they inspire others and become happier, healthier, and more successful and confident in the process.

Georgina has a proven track record in the field of people-development and has worked with large corporations in the UK and internationally to help them to get the best out of their people.

Georgina was at a ladies' entrepreneurship conference in New York in 2013 when she realised why she'd been put on this planet: to connect people and turn lights on!

Her concept and practice TLO *Happening* equips us with all the tools we need to create positive experiences, resulting in a positive world.

Introduction

I'm so pleased you've picked up this book. Yay, you! You're en route to living a happier, healthier, epic life.

But let me begin with a confession: I'm not a self-help guru, I don't have a magic wand, and I don't have all the answers. But what I do know is that you could be instantly happier, healthier, and more successful by unlocking the energy inside of you. Did I lose you at *energy?* Hmmm, thought so.

I'm well aware that energy is an intangible thing that makes people shudder and think of candles, crystals, and hippy-dippy chanting. To be honest, I'm not really into all that stuff either. But I *do* believe in energy – and the power it has.

Let me explain.
The energy we put out can help or hinder in an instant. It only takes a moment to inspire or upset someone, and if you're putting out no energy at all, that has consequences too.

We've all had meetings where we've left unimpressed because the other person wouldn't hold eye contact and gave off the vibe of wanting to be elsewhere.

Then there was that dinner with a partner or friend who actually seemed more interested in their phone.

It's being at a networking event when someone is looking over your shoulder as they shake your hand. And who could forget the customer-service representative who couldn't force a smile and made you feel awkward and invisible?

We've all been in those situations, and if we're really honest with ourselves, it's likely we've given out this kind of energy at some stage too.

When we're distracted, worried, or unhappy about something in our lives, it can be all too easy to look through people and have our thoughts wandering off elsewhere.

Simply by being mindful of our energy and the way we channel it, we can completely change the way we see the world and how other people engage with us.

I think the secret to having a great life is positive energy. The phrase 'positive thinking' is something we hear a lot, and this feel-good kind of energy is nuclear! It has real power. The more energy you have, the more you can make life happen for you.

Why I do what I do is simple: I love to connect with people and 'turn lights on' – TLO, between you and me.

In this book, you will hear 'TLO' many times, and it's my goal to help you learn about TLO and then live TLO. By carrying out each TLO Task, you will be inspired to get out and embrace life, inspiring others as you go and creating a positive world.

Throughout the chapters of this book, I will assist you in creating an awareness of that energy, fire, and passion – basically that X factor that makes us instantly warm to other people.

Think about the people who have inspired you in your life. Maybe it was that teacher whose enthusiasm for your education made you want to work harder; that conversation with a stranger that encouraged you to change your job; or the service from an individual that made you feel so appreciated, you are likely to be a customer for life.

How can you put out that kind of energy every day? Who can you go the extra mile for? How can you give your best and care about people? Where can you give your time to make a difference in return for nothing?

'But what's in it for me?' you may ask.

The answer is – *everything:* job satisfaction, happiness, positive daily interactions, and people reciprocating as you attract fellow superstars into your life.

It's the difference between shuffling along, feeling like the world is against you, and walking with a spring in your step, fired up by your daily interactions and excited by what could be just around the corner.

The world is waiting for *you* to be *turned on* and to *turn lights on* in others.

TLO starts from *you.*

So What Exactly Is TLO?

Turning someone's lights on means sharing a moment with someone and being fully in that moment with them.

It's connection! It's about you *both* being turned on (*Oh, dear! No, not like that!*), so you're animated, happy, living in the moment, and reaping the benefits.

It's about being the best you can be, living life to the fullest, and feeling positive and happy as you live your life right now. The simple fact is, the present is all we really have.

Let me explain by telling you an old story about Jimmy, who likes a pint.

Jimmy loves a beer, especially after a hard day's work. So imagine his glee when he notices a pub on his way home. Oh boy, it's a really lovely one! You know, one that has a cracking beer garden, a dog water bowl at the entrance, hanging baskets, and good, honest pub grub. Think less Cockney boozer and more *Midsomer Murders*!

Then Jimmy notices a sign swinging in the breeze at a rather glacial pace and can hardly believe his eyes.

FREE BEER TOMORROW!

Wowee! Jimmy is chuffed to bits. He pictures himself after work, sipping a cool beer and salivating over a hearty portion of fish and chips.

He returns the next day, all excited, thirsty, and hungry but is confused that the sign is still there, and it still says:

FREE BEER TOMORROW!

Did Jimmy get his beer? Alas not, dear readers. Why? Because tomorrow just doesn't exist.

The other 'no such days' are: one day, someday, yesterday.

We only have *now*. Today. This is the only moment to trust, to share, and to live in.

So *TLO* is about filling your life with more *now* moments, being in the now, and bringing other people with you.

Your Life Is Happening Now

What does it feel like? It feels great! You don't think; you just connect!

It's like the time when you met a friend and you looked at your watch to discover an hour had flown by, or you went for a run and covered five miles without thinking, because you were simply enjoying the fresh air, endorphins, and scenery en route.

It's that time you danced all night, laughed all night, talked all night, or shopped for hours. It's anything that makes you *happy* and connected.

What does it look like? Think of someone looking really bored, fed up, and not at all interested. Now reverse it!

When our lights are on, we look and feel brighter. You can see this in people's faces, eyes, and body posture. It's even known as 'turning it on'.

Children and animals have it in bucket-loads, and we can learn so much from all of them.

'Yeah, but children and animals haven't got anything to worry about', you may argue.

Throughout this book, we are going to talk about how to deal with worry and the things that 'mess with your mojo', so park that concern for a minute, and we will return to the troublesome subject of worry later.

For now, all you need to know is that life happens and stuff happens, and it's all down to you and how you handle it.

You can choose the happy path, passing 'Go' and picking up £200, or you could go for the misery route, straight to jail and missing out on your moolah. It's really your choice!

You can blame other people for the way they make you feel but really our reactions and the energy we put out are often the real cause.

Practising TLO is about being responsible for the things you can control and letting go of the things you can't.

What's the point of worrying over the stuff you can't change, such as the way people feel about you, their actions, or even the weather?

Surely you'd have a lot more success if you could just channel that energy positively to improve your own attitude and reactions to life.

Not only would it make you feel happier, but this kind of energy has a domino effect, inspiring other people to turn lights on too.

Positive experiences, big or small, *will* change the world.

When we make great connections and share a smile or a laugh, it is infectious.

Let me give you an example.

A Different Kind of Supermarket Challenge

When I've finished my weekly shop, I will deliberately approach the checkout manned by the sales assistant who most looks like they could do with a little increase in their wattage.

'Hello, how are you doing?' I'll ask enthusiastically while looking them straight in the eye. Then I'll spark up a conversation, usually making them laugh by being a bit random and then warmly bidding them goodbye.

Then I'll discreetly stand back for a moment and watch them interact with the next shopper. How do they seem now?

More often than not, I'll see a sparkle in their eye as they chat to their customer, and I'll skip off knowing I've cheered up their day and mine.

The total cost of that bit of fun was zero pence and minimal effort, but what a difference it makes!

That, in a nutshell, is my daily TLO mission – to turn lights on, energise people, and let them do the rest.

I see myself as a catalyst, someone who can give you a bit of guidance or mentoring, if you will. It is my goal to nudge you in the direction of your dreams – but ultimately it is down to you to make things happen.

When we can get out of our own way and stop sabotaging ourselves, that's when we can really shine.

This book will start by helping you understand and learn about the abundance of positive energy and confidence that is inside you. Then, once you've discovered the rock and roll, you can go out and share the music.

Treat this book as your go-to 'feel-good' manual, to be kept close by, read and re-read, and filled with your own notes and wisdom as you discover it.

A little message before we start.

I'm telling you my truth, my opinion that I have come to after thirty-odd years on this planet. It comes with the best intentions, so feel free to use it or disregard it as you see fit.

All I ask is the following:

- Begin with an open mind.
- Be honest with yourself.

- The book is an introduction to Turn Lights On. I could have gone into lots more depth and I will in my other books. This is just the start.
- Take Action, We are going to be powerful and surf the wave of fear, so 'try' needs to leave our vocabulary. You are either going to do it or not!
- Get used to feeling fear and start to enjoy it. It's good to feel it; it means we are growing. Don't let it stop you – *fear is your friend*.
- **The success will be your application of the practice.** The book is the start. This is very important: no book ever written has or can change a person's life; it's the action taken after reading the book that's the life-changing bit!
- Be proud of yourself. It took a great deal of blood, guts, and sweat to get you here. It's your duty to humanity to have an awesome life. I love a dramatic sign-off!

Chapter 1

Time to Change the Record

Let's get one thing straight: I don't have the secret formula to give you the perfect life, incredible success, or Donald Trump-esque riches. But I do know how to help you feel happy about everything you do have, empowered to do great things, and eager to spread your joy wide and generously.

I feel happy and enthusiastic about life. I love my work, feel proud of myself, and enjoy positive interactions with people. When I want to achieve something, I go out and do it!

'Okay, Pollyanna', I hear you say. 'That's all well and good when *you* have a sunny disposition and unwavering confidence, but that just isn't *my* default setting.'

Well, actually I'm inclined to agree. Believe it or not, all this positivity and self-belief didn't just land in my lap; it's a work in progress.

Let me take you back. A six-year-old Georgina stood in front of a class full of youngsters at school, getting all hot and bothered as she tried to write her name on the blackboard.

This was a big moment. It was the end of the term, and we were moving up to the next class. Writing your name on the board was supposed to be symbolic of this rite of passage. Only I couldn't remember how to spell my name.

After several attempts, I'd got myself into a right muddle.

'Never mind, go through', the teacher eventually told me. 'It's fine.'

Only it wasn't fine to me. I couldn't spell my name!

I remember the feeling of not being good enough when everyone else in my class was good enough. I didn't deserve to be there!

Sadly, that horrible 'inadequate' feeling stayed with me for a long time, even following me into my early thirties. I would constantly compare myself to others and never felt good enough – despite all the things I achieved. Sound familiar?

I used my problem with reading and writing to avoid it whenever I could, relying on the phone instead of e-mail and viewing spell-check as one of my best friends.

After school, I went on to do performing arts, but despite being blessed with a good singing voice and a passion for acting, I'd often get into a real panic about reading an unfamiliar script. Inevitably my hands would start shaking, and eventually I decided the anxiety was too much.

But when I went on to get a so-called *real* job, whilst running and hiding from my insecurities, I somehow found myself tasked with the responsibility of checking my team's e-mails and letters before they went out to customers.

Yes, that included spelling and grammar. Oh Lordy, how on earth could I do that?

I did it largely using spell-check, remembering strategies, and staying late to go over everything with a fine-toothed comb. But instead of giving myself a little high-five for all that hard work and initiative in getting the job done, I often felt I really shouldn't be in the position.

What if someone discovered how thick I really was?

'I'm so thick' was one of the records I constantly played in my head. I'd taken one weakness and made it my world.

My breakthrough moment came a few years ago, when I discovered something wonderful about myself: my difficulty with reading and writing was all due to dyslexia!

Tests confirmed I had a reading age of fourteen and a writing age of seven. What a relief! Suddenly I didn't feel stupid anymore and was ready to accept and feel proud of myself.

Now I was ready to reach for the stars – to unleash the real Georgina in all her flawed beauty!

So what happened?

Being diagnosed with dyslexia hadn't suddenly morphed me into a spelling whiz, yet in the twinkling of an eye, it had dramatically helped my self-esteem and confidence. I stopped calling myself 'thick', and instead I embraced my talents and achievements.

It made me examine what other parts of myself I'd allowed to be overshadowed because I'd focused on a weakness and overlooked the good stuff. Why had I been stuck for so long, wishing and longing to be someone else? What a giant waste of time!

I often think back to the woes of child George, teenage George, and twenty-something George and send them all a little hug.

These days, I follow Oscar Wilde's mantra: 'Be yourself, because everyone else is taken.'

TLO also stands for *to love oneself*.

So my breakthrough came when I changed the record from 'I'm thick' to 'I have a gift'.

Imagine your brain as a record player and your thoughts as vinyl records. You put all sorts of vinyl on, depending on whatever mood you are in. The lyrics are the messages that make you feel a certain way.

So, pop pals, what are you listening to at the moment? How is your music making you feel? What features heavily on your playlist?

Is it the *'I can do this'* power ballad? Or is it the *'I can't do this'* song? Are you singing along to the *'I deserve this'* feel-good track? Or is the *'What am I doing? Everything goes wrong for me'* tearjerker stuck in your head?

What I'm doing is describing your 'self-talk', the way you speak to yourself all the time.

First thing in the morning, what are you saying to yourself? What's your 'song' when you are stepping into the shower or looking in the mirror? Is it the *'I'm looking good today'* jam, or are you warbling along to the sad strains of *'I wish I looked twenty years younger'*?

All these songs make a difference to your day, and your self-talk is so powerful that it shows in your face, posture, and the energy you put out.

Think of the effect music has in a bar, a restaurant, or a dinner party; it can instantly lift or lower the mood. I know we don't sing our thoughts, but the impact is still the same.

If you have a really sad song playing, how are you going to turn someone's lights on? How are you going to feel good?

What songs are playing for you right now?

As I've told you, two of mine used to be *'I know I'm a bit thick'* and *'I'm not clever enough to do that'*.

In fact, I got so used to hearing those records that I still sing the words from time to time – until I make a concerted effort to change the record.

I know the words to the songs that don't serve me, but I still have to be careful that I don't catch myself singing along mournfully on autopilot when faced with fear. It's about being aware of what's playing.

It's time to have a good sort through that old vinyl, to see which anthems make you feel great and identify the sad songs holding you back.

Think about what you want to hear about yourself and what makes you feel amazing. If it starts with 'I can't' or 'I should', change that record to 'I can' and 'I could'.

The whisper in our ears, the stuff that happens in the background, the deep, engrained messages that we tell ourselves seep into our brains, creating our reality. If that message is largely critical, it's time to change the record.

You may need a hand with identifying these songs, so you could always enlist the help of someone who loves and cares about you as you carry out the following exercise.

TLO Task: What's on Your Playlist?

- What kinds of things do I say about myself?

- How do I describe myself?

- When I do something new, what do I say to myself before I do it?

- What do I say to myself when I walk into a room full of strangers?

- How do I feel when I look in the mirror?

- What things do I say about my body?

- What do I say about my life?

Now have a look at what you said.

Are these songs inspiring you? Are the words empowering or critical? Are they making you feel you can turn people's lights on, or are they turning *your* light off?

Once you've identified the songs that are not working for you, have a think about creating some new songs.

Here's a tip: take anything that is not making you feel great and reverse it. For example: 'When I look in the mirror, I think I look old' could be changed to 'When I look in the mirror, I look at me: one-off, unique me. No one is like me; I'm a complete original. Age is a gift that is given to few.'

Changing the song to a more positive message is much cheaper than cosmetic surgery.

I know this sounds very easy, but it's as hard or as easy as you think it will be! Changing songs takes time, and at first, you are going to feel a bit odd. A new album has to grow on you, so you can't expect to listen to it once and know all the lyrics. However, if you stick with it, soon you'll be singing along as if you've known the words all your life.

Write all your new song titles here:

Life is too short to listen to bad music, so enjoy this process, have fun, and remember that the voice in your head should work *for* you, not *against* you.

Your self-talk is with you constantly, so imagine spending time with someone constantly who was putting you down and pointing out all the areas you need to improve on. Would they be on your Christmas card list? I doubt it!

You deserve to hear the best things about you, so change the record and enjoy your listening.

Chapter 2

Buy This Book and Get a Free Guru!

So, back to that Pollyanna accusation …

Just like everyone, I have days that make me want to headbutt my desk, curl up into a little ball, or stress-gulp gin and tonic. Even when I've changed the record, I still have moments when I feel conflicted or unsure of which way to go. That's what life is like, an exhilarating roller-coaster of ups and downs.

But did you know the person to help you get past that feeling is right under your nose? When brain fog or melancholy creeps in, it's time to call in the crème de la crème – your guru!

I like to think of my guru as a Zen-like monk – a female version of the Dalai Lama who sits in my tummy, floating on a cloud and looking very wise and of course guru-like!

My guru is always there waiting for a question, ready to give me the answer. She doesn't speak, as she is a silent monk, but if I really listen, I get the messages in the form of feelings. She's the best friend who knows exactly what's right and wrong for me.

She knows the people I should spend time with and the people who are not the best fit for me. She warns me when I'm in danger and gives me a little push when I need it. She has my journey all mapped out, like a little satellite-navigation device, guiding me closer to my goal. We're going to be friends for life.

'It's that easy?' I'm pretty sure you just scoffed. 'I just tune in to my guru?'

Well, yes and no.

Sadly, your guru isn't going to magically float to life with a flourish of 'Namaste'.

In order to unleash the guru, there is a little work to be done, and first and foremost it starts with trust. What I actually mean is learning to trust your intuition, your inner voice – that feeling in your gut. It's the niggle we ignore a lot of the time and then beat ourselves up after the event for not paying attention.

It can be hard to tune in with so much external noise, but it pays to remember that often, deep down, the answer we really need is there inside of us. Perhaps it is not the *firm* answer, but it is a little spark, a small step towards the answer.

In her bestselling book, *Eat, Pray, Love*, Elizabeth Gilbert talks of lying on the bathroom floor, crying night after night because she felt unhappy in her marriage and didn't know what to do. Her eureka moment finally came when she started to hear her inner voice, which simply told her, 'Go back to bed, Liz'.

It wasn't a breathtaking message; it didn't suddenly mend everything – but it was still good advice nonetheless. By going back to bed and looking after herself, Elizabeth could begin to find the energy to work through some difficult life decisions – which she ultimately did, all by herself.

Listening to other people's logic is something we all do, but while having support is important, no one else can ever really know what is best for you; that is something only you will discover.

Living your own journey is very important; nobody sees and feels the world exactly in the same way you do. While it can seem scary, ultimately you have to trust yourself.

My close relationship with my guru really began in my thirties. Before that, we knew of each other but were not really friends, so to speak. Back in my twenties, when I still didn't like or believe in myself enough, I didn't always give her the time of day. Although I could sometimes feel my guru telling me, 'Don't do that! You'll regret it!' I didn't really listen.

The disadvantages of not being mates with my guru meant that I felt a little lost at times. It's a shame, as really, I had all the answers. I don't mean 'all the answers' in a conceited way, more a case of all *my* answers.

I suppose the connection with my guru came when I got to a place where I decided to take a leap of faith and trust my intuition. At the time, I was working for a big insurance company which is known for being an excellent employer – and it really is a wonderful company. I had the most fantastic time working and travelling internationally for them.

Having left school with a handful of GCSEs and no degree, I'd worked my way up the corporate ladder and was in a great position to stay and develop within the group. Yet my guru was shouting for me to leave! I had an urge to explore and do something that stretched my creative talents.

Although I attempted to ignore my guru – and even tried to pacify her by taking a career break to Spain in the summer of 2008 – it was no good. When I returned to work, my guru had turned into a noisy neighbour. I call it 'the feeling', and trust me, there is no amount of handbags, glasses of wine, or holidays that can cure 'the feeling'.

Unable to ignore her any longer, I decided to leave my fantastic job and develop a creative idea for my first business. Somehow, I just knew that my guru had my back! I trusted my belief that everything would be okay and figured that if it went wrong, it would make an interesting dinner party story!

Luckily for me, it did all work out. Yes, it was hard and scary from time to time, but I was on track to my dreams. I was feeling a mix of emotions every day. I think that's what I love about my life: being *alive* – whether it's feeling love, joy, or fear, I'm alive and awake.

I'm very proud of the first business I created. It does wonderful things and makes such a difference in people's lives, so going for my dream paid off. Even if the business was unsuccessful, I'm sure the lessons I would have learnt would have led to somewhere. Everything leads to somewhere when you keep on moving; it's when you stop then that you have a problem.

Let change happen, as it's going to happen regardless; accepting it and inviting it is far less painful, as change is inevitable.

Learning to listen to your guru is a bit like learning a language: the more you work on it, the more you grow to understand.

There is nothing worse than feeling overwhelmed and confused, but the more you tune in to your guru, the easier it will become to make decisions and feel empowered that you are doing what is right for you.

It's important for me to acknowledge that during times of stress, it can be hard to find that guiding voice. But it's all about taking small steps and not expecting the Dalai Lama to appear in a jiffy.

The best way to begin to connect with your guru is by being kind to yourself. The relationship with yourself is the best and the most important relationship you will *ever* have.

Then, moving forward with patience and compassion for yourself, you can begin to work on your Guru Practice.

TLO Task: Guru Practice

1. Ask yourself a question. *(Maybe not in public, as people may not understand you are having a conversation with your guru!)*

Consider a question about your life in your mind and see how that makes you feel. At first, you may feel like a giant fool, but trust me, soon you will start to feel the answers.

For example, whenever I watch TV (which is rare) I ask myself, 'How is this really making me feel?'. Then I start to feel the answer. If a depressing show is making me gloomy, then it's time to turn off the goggle box. Feeling the answer is often the best thing we can do and sometimes the only thing that makes sense.

2. Get to know yourself. I am a *huge* believer in keeping a journal or diary. Make an effort to write something every day, and remember to write about your feelings. *'Went to work and it was boring!'* doesn't tell you much. However, if you wrote that every day, it would tell you that you may need to change your job.

Write about situations – what makes you happy, why you did what you did, and how it made you feel. I often make a note of what exercise, food, and drink I've had that day, to see if that's been a factor.

After a month, look back at your notes, and prepare to be enlightened. Just four weeks of journaling can show you what your life is *really* like, what works for you, and what needs to change.

As Stephen King says, 'I write to find out what I think.'

You'll definitely know when you *weren't* listening to your guru!

3. Spend some time sitting, resting, being in nature, and relaxing to reconnect.

When you sit still and really begin to see and hear what's going on around you – whether that be birdsong, the distant hum of traffic, or lapping of the ocean or a river – it helps shut off all the thoughts spinning around your mind.

This is your chance to strengthen the connectivity lines between you and your guru.

When I give myself time out to think, I often remember the Serbian proverb, 'Be humble for you are made of earth, be noble for you are made of stars', to get some perspective.

Meditating may seem like a mission; however, it's a great opportunity to mute the noise of life and spend some quality time with your guru. Studies have shown that meditation can reduce anxiety and depressive symptoms.

You could try a meditation class or just download a phone app with relaxing music and meditation exercises.

Just sitting down in silence for five minutes a day can help. We can all spare five minutes!

4. Go for a walk or run, and spend some alone time to give yourself space and enjoy some quality time with your guru. As with all relationships, you need to talk, and the more you communicate, the stronger your relationship will be!

5. Try a yoga class to connect your mind and body. As you concentrate on breathing and stretching, your mind will take a welcome break from the daily grind. With your worries and strife silenced, your guru will be able to speak clearly.

I find that swimming works well too, but everyone is different – find your thing.

6. Get creative. What made you happy as a child? Drawing, painting, singing, or dancing? Do something that turns your light on. Your guru very much approves of you doing stuff you love.

7. Be patient. When I'm stressed and not feeling my guru, it seems easy to give up; persevere with all these exercises until you start to get the message loud and clear. I also find this quote inspiring: 'When your mind is full of indecision, try thinking with your heart.'

Your relationship with your guru is one of the most important relationships in your life, so what are you waiting for? Put this book down and introduce yourself to your guru.

Have a chat, and magic will start to happen. I promise! Be patient, actually just *be!*

Chapter 3

What's Your Excuse?

In 2013, I decided to tick off a gruelling challenge on my bucket list – running the London Marathon. Prior to this, the only race I'd done was a half marathon. While I could comfortably get around the 13.1 mile route without getting acquainted with St John's Ambulance, I was no Paula Radcliffe.

It was clear I had some serious work to do – long training sessions before work and epic runs at the weekend in the cold, wind, and rain. While the training was intense, what was even more of an uphill battle was pacing past all the excuses why I shouldn't be doing the marathon – not just from me but from a bunch of doomsayers as well!

People love to tell you how dangerous it is, how they could never do it, that it is not natural to run that far, and how you must be careful not to injure yourself.

All of this, while well-meaning, is not exactly helpful when you already have a little voice in your head making excuses that you don't have time to train or it is too boring to do or a million other justifications to talk yourself out of running.

As if my internal battle to stay motivated wasn't enough, I blinking went and injured myself and came down with a bladder and kidney infection the week before the marathon.

I could have easily used any of those excuses not to run; however, I was determined to do it and to finish, and finish I did.

The moral of the story is you can talk yourself out of everything! So watch out you don't start believing your own excuses and renaming them as reasons. There will always be excuses *not* to do things, but your mind-set and attitude are the underlying influences that help you get to where you need to be.

Intention is the mother of it all. If your intention is to do it well, then you will. Likewise, if deep down you are feeling half-hearted, you'll find an excuse to walk away. It's really your choice.

Excuses are something that pop up a lot in our daily conversations. If we have a reason for doing or not doing something, it makes us feel ever so much better, doesn't it?

'I've had a terrible day and I need a glass of wine!'
Suggestion: You don't *need* anything – just have a glass of wine if you want a glass of wine.

'I'd volunteer at the homeless shelter, but it's too hard, as I don't have a car to get there.'
Suggestion: If you really, passionately wanted to do it, you'd find a way to get there via public transport.

'I'd love to exercise. I just haven't got the time, with work and my family.'
Suggestion: If you love something, you do it because you love it; you make it a priority!

When we think about it, there are lots of excuses we feed ourselves:

- *You need money to do that.*
- *I'm too old for that; maybe if I was younger.*
- *If I had a better education …*
- *If I had my time again …*
- *I haven't got time for that.*
- *It's hard in this financial climate.*
- *I did that before I had kids.*
- *If I didn't have kids …*
- *If I had kids …*

Excuses like not having enough time or being short of money can make us feel a bit better for not doing what we truly desire, when the truth is that we are too lazy or fearful to do it.

Maybe I sound a little harsh, but who else is going to pull you up on your excuses? When you really want to do something, you just do it – don't you?

An excuse can be a way of squashing feelings of fear – almost like a bossy parent scolding, 'No no, you don't do that'. After all, it's sometimes easier to come up with a reason *not* to do something.

Often, our excuses seem like valid reasons. We truly believe these obstacles are stopping us from doing what we want to do. But if we admit that these 'reasons' are actually excuses, we have to do something about them. That leads to action and tackling fear.

When I set up my first business, the UK was on the brink of recession, and everyone said I was an idiot to leave a secure job to follow a dream. But I had to put that fear aside and trust that unrelenting intuition from my guru, the one that said: 'follow your feelings and your dreams will come.'

It would have been very easy for me to believe my own excuses and stay safe, coasting along in a good job. However, that wouldn't have been very fair on me or the company I was working for.

When friends talk to me about why they can't do something, I say, 'Do you want me to be your mate, or do you want me to be your coach?' If they go with the mate option, I just listen and nod, as it's nice to give them a chance to let off steam (although I'm always dying to wade in and help).

If they go with the coach option, I highlight how all their so-called reasons are excuses. I must be an annoying friend sometimes, but it all comes from a place of love. I really want to help them.

I will tell them (and you) this for nothing – being 'realistic' about your dreams and expectations for yourself is far too predictable and makes for a rather boring story.

I once saw an interview with Will Smith where he said, 'Being realistic is the most common path to mediocrity.' I could have kissed that man!

Creating electricity, putting a man on the moon, and a plane taking you across the world were not realistic at one time, but look where we are now! Thank goodness for people who think in an unrealistic way!

So I challenge you to be unrealistic.

Push aside all the reasons why you can't do something, and imagine if you actually could. What's the worst that could really happen?

When I take risks – mainly financial risks – my 'worst thing that could happen' is losing everything I own and living back home with my parents. That, to me, isn't really so bad. They have a lovely home, and I love spending time with them, so really, I have nothing to lose.

Likewise, a friend of mine named Louise, who has a family and wanted to leave her corporate job to become a reflexologist, found her way to take that leap. The final reassurance she needed came from her best friend, who happily agreed that if it all came to nothing and they fell upon hard times, Louise and her family could live with her as a temporary measure. Louise was able to try something new securely, and now she is doing what she loves.

At the end of the day, it's the big stuff that matters – having your health and the people you love around you. These are the most important things; the rest is just 'stuff'.

If you lose the attachment to things, life is a whole lot more fun.

Now reread that sentence!

Your stuff does *not* define you – who you are as a person defines you; your actions and your intentions, not whether you have a forty-two-inch television. I always remember talking to my mother about wanting a new carpet for my apartment but also wanting to go on holiday. She said, 'George, when you are ninety years old, looking back on your life, you will think of the experiences you had, not if you had a beautiful carpet.'

Needless to say, I went to Ibiza and spent enough for several carpets!

TLO Task: Excuse Practice – *Are you ready to put your pure honesty hat on?*

- What are the things you want to do now that you are not doing?

- What are the reasons why you are not doing it? (Go for it; write as many as you can think!)

- Now have a look at the list and see which of the 'reasons' are really excuses.

- Now consider: what is the worst that can happen in your world if you actually think big and make it happen?

I hope you enjoyed that exercise! We all have boundaries and people who rely on us, but I encourage you not to make other people your excuses too.

You will always cope if you want it enough and you love what you are doing. You are your first priority; take care of yourself and then move on to inspiring others.

I will say it again: follow your feelings and your dreams will happen.

Chapter 4
The Slippery Matter of Your Ego

When we think about people with a big ego, we often think of larger-than-life people who love to speak their minds, demand the limelight, and don't seem to care what anyone thinks of them. But it's a little bit misleading to simply palm off big egos on the rich, power-hungry, rambunctious, and famous. Actually, a lot of everyday people have more than an ample dose of ego, and I'd hazard a guess that you are one of them. Yes, *you!*

Think about the part of you that wants to be liked, accepted, or be in with the in-crowd. The little voice that asks questions like …

- *But what will people think of me?*
- *What happens if I look silly?*
- *What happens if I don't fit in?*
- *Why hasn't my boss told me how great I am today?*
- *Why has no one liked my Facebook status yet?*

Your ego is basically a needy friend, that insecure pal who always needs reassurance or for you to call them and tell them how great, funny, and intelligent they are or how wonderful they look or that they are the most important person in the world.

It's exhausting, especially if you're with this person 24/7; they always want more attention and are too preoccupied with their own dramas to care about anyone else.

Your ego is basically a greedy monster, and the more you pander to it, the more insatiable its appetite becomes.

It is because of the ego that we don't always try new things, embrace our creative side, or trust in ourselves. It's the feeling of being caught out, being busted, or someone working out that you are – God forbid – human!

The fact is, as humans we do make mistakes, and we can't be right all the time. The only way to get past the ego is to accept our imperfections, shake it off, and dust ourselves down.

Basically it's about losing your inhibitions a little and summoning up a childlike spirit for adventure. Think about all the times a child falls down while learning to walk. There are so many knocks and scrapes, but children get up and keep on going.

There is no little voice saying:

- *Don't fall; you will look stupid!*
- *Walk perfectly, you idiot!*
- *Quick, get up before anyone sees!*

Do you remember the last time you fell in public? Chances are, you leapt up again like a startled cat and tried to pretend it hadn't happened. Then you walked off, trying your best not to limp, sporting a bright-red face and a humiliated feeling in your tummy. But your five-year-old, ego-free self would not have cared that much!

The ego can also control the way you handle situations and treat other people.

A friend of mine, Eleanor, works in a busy TV studio and once sat on the desk next to a woman who had numerous staff members. This colleague's favourite pastime was to scold her staff in public. Eleanor would often walk into the newsroom to see her standing in a very public place, telling one of her trainees, 'I could sack you right now, you know.'

It always struck Eleanor that these public shows were not about teaching her staff to do better or not to make mistakes but to exercise her authority and self-importance in front of everyone else. If her real motivation was to teach her trainees to do better, why not take them into an office and explain properly and privately?

The trouble is we are encouraged by society to have egos: *Because you're worth it! You must be someone! I* am *someone – I'm* me! But there is a fine line between believing in yourself and pandering to the ugly side of your ego. Think of all the trouble your ego gets you into on a daily basis. When was the last time you felt self-important or reacted from a place motivated purely by what other people think of you? Was it really worth it? How did it really make you feel?

Years ago, I had my handwriting analysed for a promotion at work, and the first line read: 'The subject has a rather large ego.' *What?* I was shocked, and so was my rather large ego!

Whether I wanted to hear it or not, I did have a rather large ego. At the time, I thought it was a good thing, as I assumed that having an ego was about style, personality, and confidence.

Letting go of my ego is one big daily journey, a life's work – and I'm still on it, and will be for many years to come. But the more I have learnt to let go of my ego and spend time with people who are not driven by theirs, the more freedom has started to come.

I have a beautiful friend named Aimee who creates many YouTube videos to do with her business, and while she has received some wonderful comments, she's definitely gotten some not-so-wonderful ones too. However, learning to let go of her ego when she reads the mean things people occasionally write is a way to keep sane. She realises that the comments are based on other people's thoughts, feelings, and – more importantly – reality.

Aimee and I are both big fans of the book *The Four Agreements* by spiritualist author Don Miguel Ruiz, which talks about not taking things personally. This book was a real turning point for me. I finally realised that letting go of my ego gives me freedom, and freedom is my biggest driver.

After reading about 9 million self-help books and learning from life, I have come to realise that my ego can be the one thing that gives away all my power.

The ego relies on other people, what they say about you, how they feel about you. So you spend your whole time giving your power away, waiting for the next comment – or compliment – to influence your mood, motivation, and what you think of yourself.

Next time you feel your ego creeping out to demand attention, try asking yourself the following questions.

TLO Task: Taming the Ego-Monster

- What outcome am I looking for? What do I desire, and are my actions reflecting my desires?

- What is my real motivation for doing this? What is fuelling my intention to do this?

- Is being right really going to make me happy? What will it give you apart from the knowledge of being right?

- What do I really want ?

- Does being right really matter?

- Is this the best route to my end goal?

- Where will be 'being right' actually get me ?

You can't keep your ego down all the time. Inevitably, you'll have a battle to keep the naughty little chap caged on occasion, but you can also learn to recognise when it is in danger of escaping and take the decision not to feed it.

We all like to be right, and we all want respect from our peers, but the only person who controls how you feel about yourself is *you*. Really, it's feelings of respect and connection we want, and we have an abundance of that within us if we keep our egos in check.

Some of the most splendid people I've met in life are those who keep their ego trim, laugh at themselves, go with the flow, and have a healthy dose of self-esteem. Unlike the ego monster, self-esteem is about quietly knowing and accepting yourself. Self-esteem is like a friend you enjoy being with, one who is enthusiastic and excited by life, who shares good things with you and isn't offended if you don't call him every five minutes.

This BFF has a healthy attitude to mistakes, preferring to be philosophical and not beating himself up when things don't quite go to plan. In fact he is the first to tell you how he tripped on the pavement and have a good laugh at his silliness.

TLO Task: How to Hang Out with Your Friend Self-Esteem

- Find a place that has lots of people in it, and do a spot of people-watching. Look at the way they walk. What are they doing? Are their lights on? Do they look happy? Think about what their lives may be like. This is not an exercise in judgement; it is just a way of understanding that everyone has stuff going on. The term 'first-world problems' sums it up beautifully. Yes, someone being short with you at work is frustrating, but in the grand scheme of things, it probably wasn't about you. People do things because of what is going on in their own lives, so don't take it all so personally.
- Get out of your own way; write down how you are feeling and clear the air. If you write a letter to a person, you don't have to give it to them; just get those emotions and feelings out. Sleep on it, have a read afterwards, and see if you still feel as strongly. Chances are, you will feel calmer and more rational, and you won't let your ego rule the situation.
- Turn someone's lights on. This is my personal favourite. When it's all about you, make it about someone else! Stop obsessing, and use that energy to help, volunteer, or do something for someone else. You will instantly feel

better, and it's likely that very important thing will suddenly not feel as important!
- Climb a hill or mountain and look at the scale of the world. We spend a lot of time thinking that we are the only person in the world. I use nature to see that each of us is merely a tiny speck! It really helps me to see I am part of a bigger picture - it's not all about me!
- Listen to someone inspiring. I love listening to Wayne Dyer, a wonderful speaker and self-help author who has really helped me to understand my ego. As he says, 'An ego is a wave that thinks it is an ocean.' The more you read and explore this subject, the more inspired to change for the better you will become!
- Think about the last disagreement you had, and imagine if you didn't have to be right. That can be uncomfortable, especially when you really want to feel self-righteous, view that other person as the enemy, and feel hard done by. But are your principles just a massive way of justifying your ego? While having standards and beliefs is admirable, keeping hold of your principles can sometimes stop you from listening and can cause you to be unnecessarily judgemental or stubborn. Having a principle with an underlining theme of 'I want to do good and turn lights on' works much better.

Would it matter if you had just one more day to live? This is a question I ask myself all the time. The highly talented James Dean said, 'Dream as if you'll live forever, live as if you'll die today.'

In one hundred years all of us will most likely be dead. Think about that, really think about it. A healthy dose of mortality can be a real incentive to live your best life now and forget all about those 'principle' ego trips.

Chapter 5

The Truth about Toxic Energy

We live in a world where people often slip into autopilot.

We run from place to place, feeling fraught and pressured, always consumed by the next thing on our agenda and unable to enjoy the moment or the magic of our lives. When we are stressed, rushed, annoyed, or grumpy, it is easy to find fault with other people.

- *Why is that stupid person hogging the middle lane? Learn to drive!*
- *How long does it take to change a receipt reel at the checkout? I don't have time for this!*
- *It's only a cappuccino! Why is it taking so long?*

When you allow this kind of energy to consume you, it can feel toxic. Everyone around you can feel the dark cloud over your head, and whether you glare or frown or snap, you could easily transfer it to the next person you meet. Energy, whether positive or negative, is highly contagious. Not only is your mood likely to impact on the other person's morning, you're doing plenty of damage to your own day as well.

Our actions cause reactions, and what you give out, you can expect to get back again. If you treat people badly, use an aggressive or annoyed tone to your voice, or display angry body language, it's all asking for a similar reaction from others.

Taking responsibility is key; all of your actions have an effect. If you want to improve your life with TLO, you have to take responsibility. If you feel frustration and anger threatening to bubble over, then you need to neutralise it. Find a way to press the pause button, take a deep breath, and get back in control.

Twelve Steps to Calm

1. Insist on emergency peace talks with your guru; he or she will have the answer.

2. Change your mood; avoid people and places that will make you feel worse.

3. Get grateful! Gratitude is one of the first things that can propel me back to feeling great. I have a 'love list' on my phone that I read whenever I need to turn my light up. On it, I have listed everything I am grateful for in no particular order:

My parents, my family, my healthy body, my car, my freedom to make my own choices, my ability to do good, my energy levels, my education, my creativity, my singing voice, my home, holidays, the abundance of food and water I have in my life. What's on your list?

4. Listen to some music you love or sing a song. Either of these will lift your spirits swiftly.

5. Laugh at something; there are a few situations that have happened in my life that can instantly make me laugh when I think of them.

For example, whenever I need a lift, I think about getting the train to London with my friend Mel. En route, we had a few gin and tonics, and when Mel returned from the toilet, she was a bit unsteady as the moving train swayed. Lo and behold, she accidentally fell into a rather compromising position with an equally surprised gentleman. That memory always makes me laugh. Sorry, Mel!

6. Get on the Internet and watch some TED Talks. TED is a nonprofit organisation devoted to spreading ideas, usually in the form of short, powerful talks. Being inspired is the perfect antidote to a black mood.

7. Text a friend to say something short and nice; I find that just writing something nice is instantly uplifting.

8. Don't dwell, but observe however you feel. You may need to stay in this place for a bit, so I find it's good to think of yourself as a character in a book or film. What would you say to yourself if you could? Build a bridge to get over it.

9. Stop making excuses. Someone can only press your buttons if you let them; if you don't agree with this, then turn back to our little chat about egos!

10. Stay away and work through it. Sometimes I need to spend some time on my own, soak in the bath, or just sit and work though something. This will happen when you are in emergency peace talks with your guru.

11. Tweet something nice.

12. Look at a picture or a place that makes you feel good.

Being turned on to positivity is a choice, a lifestyle that makes you feel great. It's about awareness – being in the know about how bright or dim you are feeling and doing something about it.

It's down to you to check you've left the lights on. If you need to change the bulb, do it quickly.

Energy Zappers

Along with knowing what sparks great energy in me, over time I've come to realise there are also things that affect my light, so I either avoid them completely or moderate my usage of them. Here are some of the main offenders.

Television. I know that this is not going to sit well with many people, but if I want to have a life filled with passion and energy, sitting and watching the box for hours a week is not going to get me closer to my goal. For that reason, I have deliberately made watching TV difficult in my home. I have a small, no-frills TV and my sofa is vintage from the 1940s, when 'chilling out' on sofas was not really the nation's pastime, so I can last no more than an hour loafing on the couch.

Don't get me wrong; I do watch TV. However, I don't watch telly that makes me feel bad. I don't watch the news. Instead, I get all the current affairs I need from bite-size chunks from Twitter and reliable, trusted sources. I feel I'm connected but not dwelling. I am informed about the world, but I decide how I receive that information. Watching negative stories does not make me feel like I want to turn people's lights on. Instead, I watch programmes that are funny, inspiring, and interesting. Next time you tune in, ask your guru how it feels and whether it's good for you. You'll soon know the answer.

Negative music. I respond extremely well to music because I love it very much. For that reason, the wrong music can really affect my light. If I'm filling my mind up with hate, some of that is going stay there, so instead my playlists are upbeat, happy, and empowering.

Trashy magazines. While they are a guilty pleasure for many of my friends, gossip mags are just not for me. I find the body-image obsession and other messages in there can turn my lights off and trigger some old records. I'm not listening to that collection anymore, so instead I read publications filled with positive stories and messages.

Not exercising. I love to move, and being fit really gives me loads of positive energy. I see myself as a kinetic watch – I need to move to gain even more energy. I exercise most days, and I find it a very powerful thing to do. I used to exercise to lose weight, but now it's to be fit and to feel powerful. Everything I do, I put a positive intention behind it. Losing weight isn't something that motivates me, as it feels like I have loads of work to do, but being inspired by exercise-induced endorphins and the feeling of being healthy and happy is perfect.

Bad diet. I've recently discovered the impact food can have on my mood and energy levels. I'm no food expert, but I do know that keeping a food diary will give you a clear idea of how the foods you eat affect your body and mind.

Even doing this for a week will show you what agrees with you and what doesn't. If you want to explore this further, there are many books and apps out there to help you. Lately I've been monitoring my sugar intake and have really noticed how coffee, booze, and sugar all have an effect. I'm not professing 'Give everything up; my body is a temple', but what I am saying is that it's important to think about cause and effect.

I have gone through times in my life when I felt I had been drinking too much wine or gin, and there was always a reason why. We say it's because we like it. That may be true, but *why* do we like it? What is the feeling it is giving us? All I know is the more toxic stuff that goes into my body, the harder it is to hear my guru.

Too little water. I love this stuff. Water makes such a difference, helping me to focus and to feel energised. Herbal tea is a great way to sneak some water in. If you take a one-litre bottle to work and fill it up twice, you've had your daily intake – job done.

Negative people. Sometimes you have to see and deal with people who are not really into the TLO Happening and may never be ready for it. We have to accept that. Choice is everyone's entitlement, but it's then down to you how you deal with that energy.

Misery loves company, and there are plenty of emotional vampires ready to suck your energy dry. Instead of giving them power, let it wash over you, and be aware of how they will try to hook you into the drama.

I like to think of it as someone throwing you a ball. You can either catch the ball and throw it back and start to play the long game, or you can choose not to pick up the ball. Let them dribble and slam-dunk that ball to their hearts' content, but sit this one out on the sidelines.

TLO Tasks

- Your gratitude list. *Once you've written this, it will be a lovely thing to refer back to regularly. I add to mine all the time.*

- Funny therapy. *What memories make you chortle? Get them down on paper.*

- Music that makes you feel rockin'. *What songs make your soul sing? It's time to compile that playlist.*

- The 'bleurgh' list. *What are the things/people/places that affect your light in a negative way?*

Chapter 6

The Fear Factor

We all feel fear; it is an inevitable part of life as we take risks to move forward and pursue our dreams.

I'm actually feeling fear now in my life. Setting up the TLO Happening, walking away from a beautiful business with a fantastic team and amazing customers to a new idea and vision to turn lights on in the world is slightly terrifying.

When I speak to people, they say to me, 'Nice idea, George, but where is the money going to come from?'

A question like this could easily feed my fear, but I have been making a conscious decision to have it fuel my passion instead. How? Well, being paralysed by fear isn't going to help me, so instead I try to break the feeling and my concerns down.

I recognise it; accept it; act on it.

How exactly do you recognise fear? Of course, it can be masked in reasons and excuses – just like we mentioned in the previous chapters. It can also make us feel trapped into doing things that don't make us happy.

I'm too old. I haven't got enough money. I haven't got time. These are all reasons not to do something. If you find yourself using reasons like these, think *why?* Why can't you do it? What is really stopping you? What's the worst that can happen? What is doing nothing doing for you? How does it feel to be paralysed by fear?

Worry is a giant waste of time, a useless exercise that has no purpose at all. Worry leaves you trapped in the system – trapped between recognition and acceptance: *The more you worry, the less you do. The more you do, the less you worry.*

What is worry stopping you from doing? Once you've accepted your worries and concerns, you can get past that feeling.

Maybe it will take a little time for your guru to give you the answers you need, but instead of hanging around in that barren land of cups of coffee, sleepless nights, and anxiety, you can be proactive and make peace with the situation.

When I find myself in a place of worry, my aim is not to let it fester. Instead, I take myself somewhere peaceful and quiet and go through my eight steps to beating fear and worry.

TLO Task: How to Quit Worrying

1. Park it! Write it down. We've already talked about how putting pen to paper in your journal or typing away on your iPhone can really clear your thoughts. Write down all your fears, and tackle them one at a time. Are they really insurmountable, or were you just feeling a little overwhelmed?

2. What's the worst that can happen? Really think about it. The worst things sometimes lead us to the best destinations. Now look at the alternative – being stuck, feeling heavy and unmotivated because of your inaction. Remember what I said about living your life like it is your last day on Earth? Is giving up *really* how the story ends?

3. Talk, talk, talk! Your friends and family love you and have so much good advice, so who better to go to when you are feeling a little unsteady? They know you better than anyone, especially your strengths and weaknesses, and may just share the pearl of wisdom that helps you move forward.

4. Create a clear plan of action. When our thoughts are muddled, it is hard to know which way to turn. By sitting down and making a clear, concise plan, you will be primed and ready to take on the world. Sharing the plan is a good idea, as people can coach you on your problems. Just remember: these worries are just thoughts; you don't have to accept them.

5. Stay away from stuff that clouds your mind and makes you feel lethargic – booze, overeating, anything that masks the feeling and keeps you stuck. I'm not being judgemental here; I'm just saying you should be aware. The more aware you

are, the quicker you can solve your worries. If you're reaching for stimulants, ask yourself why.

6. Move into action! It's all about small steps. Do something that can make the issue better; there is always something you can do. It doesn't have to involve quitting your job. It could be setting up a blog, brainstorming your ideas, or swapping coffee for peppermint tea. No matter how small, it is still a step in the right direction. Rome wasn't built in a day, and neither were you!

7. Read the 'Epic' section of this book. (Don't worry, we're getting there!) and remember you are always in control of the way you feel.

8. Unleash your TLO! This is when TLO can make all the difference. Giving and paying things forward is an effective way to feel great. Worry and fear are very self-absorbed feelings, and we can all get a bit 'me, me, me' from time to time.

Burst out of that feeling by doing something for someone else. By doing something nice to make someone else feel good and turn their lights on, you are giving your guru a welcome break from all the doom and gloom. You're giving yourself a chance to recharge, re-energise, and push forward!

TLO Task: Breaking the Fear Down

- What are your top worries and fears at the moment?

- When do you think about these things?

- How do these fears and worries make you feel?

- Are there other factors influencing that feeling? *This can include tiredness, post-session depression (otherwise known as booze comedown), diet.*

- What would your life be like without these fears?

- What's the action required to say goodbye to these fears?

Worry comes in all shapes and sizes. I often hear 'I'm not happy if I haven't got anything to worry about!'

'Why?' I ask.

Does worrying make you happy? Are you addicted to worrying? What is the worry bringing you?

Heaven forbid we could just be brilliant.

After you have written your list, I want you to check it a few times a week, or even better, get someone else to, as they will be able to hold you accountable for any inaction.

By facing your fears head on and actively seeking a solution, you'll be amazed at how much weight is lifted off your shoulders. Alternatively, you could do nothing and lie there at night, thinking about all the terrible things that could happen, might never happen, or make you feel down and unhappy.

The choice is yours, my friend!

Chapter 7

The Time Is Now

I'll let you in on a little TLO secret: in order for us to share a moment, we have to be *in* the moment.

How in the world do we do that?

Well, it's all about presence. We've already touched upon how TLO is the energy we have when we connect with something or someone. I believe the more present and in the TLO moment you are, the more excellent a time you are having. But while some people are naturally more in the moment thanks to their personality or confidence levels, others struggle to stay there and really get a grip on what it means.

So how to explain?

I'm in the moment, writing this now. My hands are tapping on my keyboard at a rapid rate, and the words are flowing from my brain to my fingers. I feel I'm connected to something. I don't have to think; it just happens. The greedy ego is gone, squirreled away on radio silence. I am being true to myself and am totally immersed in the moment.

There are many things in life that make us feel that way: fishing, dancing, driving – whatever it is, that connection is wonderful.

Think about someone who is great at flirting. A great flirt makes you feel wonderful. The chemistry and connection is palpable in the air, and you are both well and truly turned on. (*Perhaps even in both senses of the word!*)

Your lights are on, the eye contact is sizzling, and you are alert and listening to each other as if there is no one else in the room. Now think of what you feel like when you don't want to talk to someone. Maybe that feeling you get when a pushy salesperson is trying everything to get you to part with your hard-earned cash. You can see this person's mouth moving, but the words are drowned out by the chatter in your head, screaming at you to tell them to shut up. At the same time, your body language is closed, as you try to keep all your energy to yourself. You don't want to give an amp of wattage away.

So what stops us giving away our energy? I was speaking about TLO at an event recently in New York City, and someone asked me, 'What takes us out of the moment and why aren't we in the moment?'

I replied, 'Fear and comfort'.

It's comfortable to keep our energy in, so no one can hurt, judge or bother us; it's easier to say nothing, look the other way, and not get into a conversation. However, living this so-called 'easy life' means you could also be easily overlooked.

Sadly, it's a habit now in most societies to keep yourself to yourself. I'll often take the time to speak to a stranger, often resulting in them reacting with shock – not because I've said something crazy but because I'm a stranger speaking to them without an agenda. (Well, a little agenda, and that's to turn their lights on.)

Look around the next time you are on public transport, and you'll see people have their heads in Kindles, books, and phones; a carriage full of people can feel like a lonely place.

Yet I recently had a wonderful conversation with a man on the New York subway about his neighbourhood, and he was very proud to tell me all about it. His lights were very much *on!* I left the carriage telling him how it was lovely to speak to someone.

I was glad he'd gone against the norm and had a good old chat!

At the end of the day, turning people's lights on is just about being you. It's not about impressing people or getting them to like you. It's about sharing your light and reaping the rewards.

My friend Charlotte was once at a wedding where she was seated at the 'odds and sods' table, where no one knew each other. Charlotte's default setting in such circumstances is to gabble, and finding the awkward silences at this table unbearable, she started chatting away to everyone, attempting to break the ice. She was faced with a reserved audience; at one point, fearing she was talking too much, Charlotte took herself off to the loo and had a word with herself to 'stop being a weirdo'.

But then, when she went back to the table, everyone seemed a lot more relaxed. Later, to her surprise, a couple at the table took her aside and thanked her for breaking the ice. They said they'd found her very interesting to talk to and would be following her career with interest!

The more we worry about being ourselves, the more energy we stand to lose – and that's energy we could be sharing.

My advice if you have a Charlotte 'self-doubt' moment in the loo is:

1. Wiggle your toes. Find that connection with yourself.
2. Take a deep breath, and fill your body with vital thinking power, oxygen.
3. *Trust!*

There's an age-old warning of being 'too nice', but what's really wrong with being open? Obviously, there are some ultra-personal things that no one needs to know about, but being open and friendly and sharing your energy wholeheartedly has an amazing effect. It makes people smile and relax and brings out their energy in return. It connects people, and stuff happens; you find out you have things in common. Maybe you've been to the same places or even know the same people.

Being nice is what TLO runs on – it's the fuel of TLO.

If you are nice and someone doesn't dig your niceness, there's no drama! For some crazy reason, when people are feeling good and shining their light, the odd party pooper pops up to burst their bubble or put them back in their box. In Wales, we call that *pissing on your chips!* This is a rubbish feeling, and when you have a short supply of confidence, this can really set you back.

But like I've said before, it's guaranteed to be something going on with them, rather than you. If you are doing your ego exercises and taming that monster, you'll be shrugging off that snub in a heartbeat. If you don't, fear not; there are plenty of book recommendations in our TLO Books section that will also help you get there.

If you are able to add 'I don't take it personally' to your feel-good arsenal, then you will be set up for life.

As author Don Miguel Ruiz says, 'Don't take anything personally. Nothing others do is because of you".

Write that quote down and put it on your fridge. It seems very simple, but you will soon realise that a great deal of conflict and misery is caused by our egos getting in the way, instead of us just sitting back and realising the truth: *'Someone has made that comment because they could be scared, jealous, confused or other reasons that are their reasons not yours.*

What people think is only their version of events; it isn't set in stone, and it can't make or break you. You are always in control; you have the power at all times. Think of it as a dimmer switch. You can increase or decrease your light. It's all down to you.

The other way to view it is we really don't give to get. If you are giving or being nice because you want people to like you, then once again you are throwing away your power instead of harnessing the good energy that comes from doing something selfless.

People can smell a rat when others are giving in an inauthentic way. You have to feel energy and it has to come from a true place to get a powerful connection.

If someone or something has hurt you, what's the life lesson? What can you do for yourself to get you to an open and altruistic place? Practice the exercises in this book, lose the ego, give out an abundance of positive energy, enjoy, and see what beauty you can make happen.

I love seeing someone's face and the connection I experience with them when I simply compliment the way they look or what they have done, or when I do something to make them feel special.

Feeling special and feeling cared for is a wonderful emotion, and it costs nothing! The poorest person in the world can give and feel rich. These days, we put such a value on things and stuff, but it's really people that make us feel and make a difference.

The best leaders do this with great style, giving someone feedback that will ensure they have a spring in their step or congratulating everyone on a group effort, rather than letting one person take all the glory. The art of being a great leader is to give! Give your time, give your support, and give your direction.

I also use giving in times of conflict. When someone is throwing up barriers, I think, *What can I give to this situation? How can I give more to this person? How can giving help?*

It could be that I just need to spend a little time reflecting on how the other person feels and understanding his or her point of view.

The other day, a friend and I went to have our hair done at a hairdresser's. When we walked in without an appointment, the lady, who was there by herself, seemed stressed and was a little short with her tone.

'I don't really like her. Shall we go?' my friend whispered.

'Let's turn her lights on!' I suggested.

By the time she'd finished my shampoo, we were laughing and joking, and my friend and I left happy.

We could have approached the situation with a negative, cold response and taken the whole thing personally. We could have then sat in silence and left the hairdresser's with our energy flatter and the lady still stressed. But by giving our energy with no attachment and agenda, we had coaxed that lady out of her bad mood.

It feels very good when you do this. If someone is not in a good place, don't follow them to that place; take them to *your* place!

So how can you break someone out of their bad, stressed mood?

- Ask them questions about themselves.
- Listen to the answers.
- Make eye contact.
- Make them laugh.
- Get them in the moment with you.

The key is to live TLO in both the good and the bad times!

Chapter 8

The Epic Case of Your Confidence!

Confidence is the one thing that everyone wants to find or have more of. Whenever I hold workshops, confidence is always mentioned, and it's a matter very close to my heart, as I suffered with finding my confidence in the past and still have a wobble from time to time.

Examining the term *lack of confidence* is a great start. There is no lack; your confidence is there – you just don't know or believe it yet. Basically, it's hiding under the surface, feeling a little suffocated by your beliefs. Beliefs are the facts we think about ourselves, and to us, they are complete truths. What you believe or feel you know about yourself determines who you are.

The good news is, if you change or challenge your beliefs, you will change your confidence. The secret to having it all is knowing that you already do.

So how *do* you change your beliefs, especially when they have been with you for so long?

I used to say, 'I want to sing like Aretha Franklin.' (Sure! Who doesn't?) But even though Aretha is an amazing and powerful singer, why would I want to sound like anyone else but myself? What's wrong with sounding like Georgina Jones?

At one time, it felt like a whole world of wrong. I would always put myself down, look for faults, and be massively affected by what people said. Even if I'd listened to ten compliments, I'd hang on to one minor criticism. I would always look for evidence to back up my belief that I wasn't good enough and find ways to put myself down. Better for me to do it first, before anyone else put me in my place, right?

At the same time, I was spending all my time searching for an antidote to feel good or someone to give me what I so desired. But until it occurred to me to look inside and empower myself, the search continued.

This time of my life often reminds me of the film *The Wizard of Oz* – not because I had ruby slippers and liked hanging out with flying monkeys and Munchkins, but because it is packed full of life lessons about believing in yourself.

When Dorothy ends up in the wonderful land of Oz, she embarks on a journey with three friends: the Tin Man, the Scarecrow, and the Cowardly Lion, who are all searching for something. The Tin Man wants a heart, the Scarecrow wishes for brains, and the Lion longs for courage. Do they get these in the end? The answer is no, but they do end up with something – validation!

Even though the man pretending to be a wizard (albeit with some major cool special effects for 1939) faked their wishes coming true, they all believed that something had changed. What they really received was a pat on the back from someone big and important, to say they were brave, intelligent, and had the capacity to love – all of which they already had but just didn't know!

Obviously, this is just a fairy tale, but I do wonder if those feelings would last for our trio. Would they need further reassurance? A wee bit of TLO?

I believe that unless we truly understand our own potential, we will always be searching for a Wizard of Oz to transform our lives, whether it's in relationships, careers, or simply day-to-day life. It's just not something anyone else can do for you; having a sense of self comes with acceptance and love for yourself.

What I'm suggesting is to follow the yellow brick road but bypass the Emerald City. Be your own wizard. The journey is where the magic happens, and understanding yourself is the adventure.

So, how much do you want it?

It takes balls and commitment and a limited amount of excuses to cultivate your inner confidence. First you've got to stop hiding in the safety zone, avoiding things that scare you.

I still get nervous before public-speaking engagements, meetings, difficult conversations, and singing performances. I am not the finished article, but I'm living proof that my strategies are effective; they work for me and for the people I have coached.

What records are you playing when it comes to your confidence? Do you encourage yourself? Do you praise yourself? Think of that little voice as your twin; would you choose to spend time with it? Does it turn your lights on?

Do you say things like …

- *That's just me?*
- *You can do that, but I can't?*
- *I'd never be able to do that?*

That's just not going to work for you, and it's certainly not getting you to your glory. In order to be epic right now, you've got to think differently. Write a list of all the things you can think of that scare the hell out of you, and just start doing those things. It could be taking swimming lessons, learning to drive, learning a language, doing your maths GCSE, going part time and spending more time with your kids, taking up kung fu, joining match.com, taking a course at night school, joining a choir, getting up to sing karaoke, rock-climbing, skiing – anything that will make you think, *Wow, I did that!*

TLO Task: List all the things that scare and challenge you.

Here's good news: doing all these things will turn your lights on and push you to realise your brilliance. Staying safe will not give you more confidence. Staying in your comfy, warm zone will keep you in the same position, which is cool if you want to have the life and the confidence levels you currently have, but I have a sneaking suspicion that you don't.

When I worked for the previously mentioned wonderful insurance company, I was always pushed to go for managerial positions. People would say, 'You should go for that job', when it had never occurred to me to apply. In my mind, the big jobs were for people with degrees, people who were much smarter than me, as the 'I'm thick' record was one of my most played.

But those mentors and colleagues saw something in me and gave me the encouragement to think big. I'm very grateful to those people now, as I got the jobs I went for and had a wonderful career working for an excellent company.

The reason I'm telling you this is because I want you to know: when we have people around us who can see our glory, we should *listen* to those people. They are seeing what we are ignoring.

When we are not listening and haven't found that knowledge in ourselves, other people can help us. People turn our lights on all the time; we just have to listen and act.

TLO Task: Project Praise

Make a list of people who have praised you, or list the kind of praise people give you. If you can't fill this in, then you probably haven't been listening. Think hard; those compliments and praise are in there somewhere!

Let me tell you a story about Neil …

Neil was working in a factory, as he had been made redundant from his design job and needed to pay his mortgage. One night, Neil and I were drinking wine in his kitchen and, like most nights with me, we started on goals and dreams. He said he had always liked stained glass and would like to be a stained-glass artist.

I immediately hit him with my default response: 'Do it!'

As I was charged with wine, I went on the Internet and found a degree course at a nearby college, which was incidentally one of the best glass colleges in the world. In less than a month, Neil was invited for an interview; then he secured a place on the course.

Within his first year, he'd had a commission from a church, and he finished his degree with first-class honours! He is now a full-time glass artist, and his pieces have been in exhibitions in Prague Castle and London. He has a growing customer base.

I remember at first Neil tried to talk himself out of the idea, using the excuses that we all use: money, other people's thoughts and opinions, and fear about his own ability. But in the end, his desire was strong enough. Neil worked his socks off, and the years he was studying involved him missing out on stuff we all like – clothes and holidays – but he carried on taking steps towards his dream.

If the desire is there, we can do anything. Change *can* happen. People talk about changing their lives, but then they say all the things that are stopping them. There is always a reason *not* to do something, and desire is the only thing that overrides it! If you want to be inspired and learn about desire, read *Alchemist* by Paulo Coelho. It's a wonderful tale of desire and many other lessons.

Don't let fear suppress your ability to do great things; never be afraid of what you really can do.

The Stifling Issue of Indecision

A lot of people tell me they think I'm lucky because I know what I want. Well, I actually feel like I'm still finding out. I know that indecision is a dilemma for many people. The feeling 'I know I don't want *this* life, but I don't know what life I want' is a common one.

Neil had a passion, but you might not have found yours. I have news: it may not find you; you probably need to search for it.

But the more we give to ourselves – and others – the more chance we will have of finding that passion. The more things we do that we love, the more things we will love. Being connected in your life's pursuits is an instant feel-good hit. Get used to feeling good, as it's addictive.

So let's start creating. Finding out what you enjoy is the first step to finding what turns your light on. Write down a list.

TLO Task:
What makes you happy?

Now that you have your list, think about the last time you did the things that make you happy. What are the excuses (you may call them reasons) why you are not doing these things you enjoy? How can you overcome these excuses?

Here's an example: 'I haven't got enough time.'

I *love* this excuse, as we create our own time. So, you can alter it to 'I'm changing my priorities'.

I love to exercise, and people tell me they haven't got time to go to the gym or work out each day. I reply, 'Make it a priority, like brushing your teeth, and you will.'

All kinds of things like this will be highlighted in the notes in this book and in your journal. You're going to get a clear photo of your life, and if you don't like the current picture, *change it* and change it now.

Transformation is a present event, not a future activity! Choose *now*, choose today; putting things off only makes us feel worse. Where in your calendar does it say *next week, one day,* or *tomorrow?* Don't be Jimmy waiting for his free beer. Today is the only time for change and turning your own lights *on!*

Now a little word about giving it away and paying it forward.

'The best way to find yourself is to lose yourself in the service of others.' —Gandhi

'Confidence is gained by giving.' —Georgina Jones
(I've always wanted to do that! Please don't think I'm trying to measure up to the mighty Gandhi.)

Bonding and forging positive interactions with people has a chemical reaction. It releases oxytocin, known as the 'cuddle hormone', which makes you feel fantastic and tops up your TLO. There are so many people around who could do with your help. Think about the friends, groups, clubs, and elderly people in your community.

Start off small; it's about being aware and thinking about what you can contribute. What skills do you have that could help someone? The best way to learn about yourself is to give. All your talents and skills will be revealed – trust me.

TLO Task: How can you help?

- What are your talents/ skills?

- How are you using them at the moment?

- Who could benefit from them?

- What's your action giving plan? How are you going to turn people's lights on?

As I said, TLO is not about sweeping, grand gestures – although knock yourself out if you want to do that. It's about the small things, the little ways you can help, the pleases and thank-yous, the eye contact, the extra little effort that will go a long way in making someone's day. As Mother Teresa said, 'Do small things with great love.'

The best bit is, you will feel ace too.

It's in all of us to give; think of toddlers. When they have something, they want to give it and share it gleefully. Giving is a totally natural thing that we do instinctively.

TLO will add colour to your day – let's create some experiences that really matter!

Think of the times in your life when you can create more TLO, day-to-day stuff like spending time with the people you care about, without your phone or the TV on; speaking to someone on the train or the bus; or making the people who serve you feel valued.

TLO Task: Spreading the TLO Love

- Think of a usual day and how you can TLO it up! What would you do?

- How would those TLO moments make you feel?

- How would they make the other person feel?

- What are your top TLO times that you've experienced already?

- When have you lit up someone's world and been left thrilled by their gratitude?

Whatever you are doing, or whoever you are seeing, be totally in the moment and make moments matter. When you are showing up in your own life, wonderful things happen.

Awareness is like being awake! Are you sleepwalking, or are you bright-eyed and bushy-tailed, creating moments that make a difference to you and the people you meet?

Paying it forward is a magical thing to do; it opens your life up to so much more, and it just starts with a hello. You don't have to be Mr or Mrs Confident; you could be Mr or Mrs Kind. If you give, you learn so much.

I volunteer in schools, and sometimes I can tell that the pupils in the class would prefer to be somewhere else, rather than listening to me. Even my energy levels aren't winning them round. These experiences are wonderful for me, as they make me work harder until I do turn lights on.

By giving, you grow, you learn things about yourself, and it feels *great*. I will say it again: confidence is gained by giving.

Chapter 9

Your Superstar Entourage

You can tell a lot about a person from his or her friends.

How do your friends make you feel? Energised, or like you need a Red Bull?

Everyone has down days, feels scared, and can have moments of negativity, but the people in our lives can make such a difference to how we feel. Being aware of that is really important.

I have a special group of people I definitely view as my superstars. They have this status as they always go the extra mile, and in turn, I do everything I can for them. I'm very grateful to have people like this in my life. If anything happens, they are there in a flash.

You may think that *superstar* is just another name for a friend. It isn't. A superstar is a tiny bit different. A superstar is someone who pushes, inspires, cares, and shares in your success.

Who is on your superstar list of people who give you the most energy, support, love, confidence, and guidance? I believe working out the people who are the best for you can help you be the best.

How to spot a superstar:

- You are very present in their company; time flies.
- They respect you.
- They are a little mini-fan of yours.
- They may challenge you in a good way.
- They promote you.
- They are there for you when you need them.
- You are there when they need you.

- They will encourage you.
- They tell you things about yourself that you may not see.
- They are honest with you – ouch!

They make you feel good; you make them feel good – *simple!*

However, don't forget the small print: you have to be a superstar as well!

If I had a list of superstars I went to but didn't also make them feel like superstars, then the balance would be all wrong. I would turn into an energy thief, sucking up all their superstar energy with no return.

It has to be a partnership, and you have to be a superstar in order to attract superstars into your life. You have to be in the club to benefit from the club.

My life would be very different without my superstars, and that is why I'm creating the movement, as you may not have superstars around you. The TLO Happening is changing that by creating a network of superstars!

How do you become a superstar?

If you've been reading this book, surely you know by now! You live, love, and give TLO. You turn people's lights on, and then you will be turned on. I am sending you lots of love, goodwill, and thanks for reading this book. I love the thought of you creating some light wherever you are.

How do you find superstars?

The *TLO Happening!* This is the aim and the beauty of what we are achieving – finding people who believe in what you believe in.

In the section, 'Life after the Book', you can look at all the ways to join and be a part of the Happening. There are loads of superstars ready to meet you and turn your light on. They come with a warm heart, a listening ear, and the most important thing: an *action plan.*

Another superstar will get you to superstar status as soon as you can get there. They will not join in with negativity; they will point out the learning and the acceptance and get you back to donning your superstar tights and cape in a jiffy!

You don't *really* have to wear a cape and tights. That's not a great look.

Get a picture of you when you were small, or draw one if you haven't got one to hand, and stick it here:

This little exercise has been inspired by my wonderful friend Louise, who is currently turning the lights on for many people in Papua New Guinea and doing a fine job.

She wrote about a time in her life when she was going through some challenging experiences, and her mum sent her a photo of her when she was starting school and said, 'Look how far you have come!'

I thought that was an important message. Sometimes we forget how much we have achieved.

Think of all the lessons you have learned, the skills you have gained, the people you have met, the places you have gone, all adding to your own personal wonderful life.

Look at the photo of 'mini-you' and be proud. What has happened has happened, and what is going to happen is in *your* hands.

Now for another little exercise.

TLO Task: The Hollywood You

- **What do people say about you when you are out of the room?** You can guess or be brave and ask people. Be honest with yourself, and write it all down.

- **Now think about what you would want them to say.**

- **Next imagine your life as a film.** Write down all the things that would make the trailer and the highlights, all the great bits.

Sit back and revel in all your best moments. Look at all the great things you have achieved.

Now write down everything you want to achieve. (This deserves two pages, so don't hold back.)

Praise for yourself is very important, as it reinforces how epic you are. I believe everyone has something to give; we are all miracles, so it only makes sense that we can create miracles. However, our expectations are so low a lot of the time that we don't really understand our own power.

Having a place to go (for instance, this page) where you can bask in your own glory reminds you what you have achieved and what you can achieve, resulting in what you *will* achieve.

Chapter 10

A Final Word

So my little introduction to TLO is nearly over.

I recognise that I could have gone into far more detail. However, to really *know* this stuff, you have to live it and be a part of the practice. Reading a book and then thinking it's changed your life for good is a crazy concept. This is why we have the Happening, which you will find out more about on the next few pages.

My aim for this book was to turn your light on, and now maintaining your light is down to you. But you won't be alone on that yellow brick road.

The awareness of TLO, and your awareness, were my first aim for this book. But small changes can make big differences, and together we will do it; together we can do anything.

Life after the Book

It's happening! TLO has begun.

Some days, we may not feel great, but that's the time to get our TLO books out, reread our individual feel-good guides, turn our lights on, and then ignite the world. I hope that now you've set out on this journey, you will recommend it to a friend or even buy them a copy. The more people who know about the TLO movement – tribe, crew, herd, posse, or whatever we fancy calling ourselves – the stronger the community becomes.

I have this vision of a positive army, armed with smiles, positive energy, and words, sweeping the world. My dream is to see TLO existing everywhere in businesses, schools, and communities throughout the world, turning the black and white into colour.

How am I going to do that? With you, my superstar, of course! I'd be privileged if you hopped aboard the TLO train and came on the ride with us. Our focus will be on giving and feeling good and living the lives we all deserve, where happiness is encouraged and supported.

Just think how the world could be. You can make the difference. It starts from us, and then we share the magic, and the wonder unfolds to reveal a turned-on world, energised with positive change and connections.

I often imagine what the world would be like if tomorrow everyone did one thing to turn someone's lights on. It would be a simple idea with amazing results!

What I would love for you to do now is share your stories of the moments you have turned on someone's lights via Twitter @tlonow or Facebook, and through the website *www.tloishappening.com*.

Use the hashtag #TLO or #makemomentsmatter.

Here are some examples:
Thank you Jeanne for our chat today, you turned my lights on #tlo
Read a great article about positive thinking today. Turned me on and I liked it #tlo
Had an inspiring chat to a lady in the line for the bus today #makemomentsmatter
Decided to smile at people on my way to work #tlo

I'm not going to turn the world's lights on – *we are!*

How to enjoy the Happening

You can find out all about the Happening on the website *www.tloishappening.com*. Sign up for the newsletter to have your lights turned on today and join us.

TLO Task: A final recap

- You are *epic!* You make a difference by your thoughts and actions every day.
- You are stronger than you think.
- Be careful of your ego; it could mess up your life.
- Listen to your own guru; he or she always knows *you* best.
- **Only listen to good records.**
- If you are stuck in the system, *break free*.
- Fear – Recognise it, accept it, act on it.
- **Turn lights on** wherever you go; be the change you want to see.
- *Feel* positive and think positive.
- *Positive feelings* are the fastest way to happiness.
- Surround yourself with *superstars*.
- TLO also means **To Love Oneself**; if you don't like something, change it.
- Stop making excuses.
- Party in the moment; it's where the magic happens.
- The secret to having it all is knowing you already do.
- Follow the yellow brick road; give with a full heart.
- We are better together.
- *Love* as much as possible and understand when loving is harder.
- *Choose to be a lighter; choose to turn lights on.*

TLO Books

For more inspiration, here are my top books for turning your light on.
The Four Agreements by Don Miguel Ruiz
The Mastery of Love by Don Miguel Ruiz
Making the Shift by Wayne Dyer
Alchemist by Paulo Coleho
Feeling Is the Secret by Neville Goddard
The Power of Now by Eckhart Tolle
Start with Why by Simon Sinek

My TLO Thank-You List

I just want to say thank you to two wonderful ladies who helped create the book. Thanks, Paula Morris and Charlotte Ward, for helping, supporting, and being brilliant!

Thank you to all the Happening for the great feedback, ideas, and support; together we will turn the world's lights on.